SHROPSHIRE SLS

January 2004

LABURNUM HOUSE

Take-OFF! Space Observer
THE PLANETS

Jenny Tesar

Heinemann LIBRARY

First published in Great Britain by Heinemann Library
Halley Court, Jordan Hill, Oxford OX2 8EJ
a division of Reed Educational and Professional Publishing Ltd.

Heinemann is a registered trademark of Reed Educational & Professional Publishing Limited.

OXFORD   MELBOURNE   AUCKLAND
JOHANNESBURG   BLANTYRE   GABORONE
IBADAN   PORTSMOUTH NH   CHICAGO

© Reed Educational and Professional Publishing Ltd 2000
The moral right of the proprietor has been asserted.

All rights reserved. No part of this publication may be reproduced, stored in a retrieval system, or transmitted in any form or by any means, electronic, mechanical, photocopying, recording, or otherwise without either the prior written permission of the Publishers or a licence permitting restricted copying in the United Kingdom issued by the Copyright Licensing Agency Ltd, 90 Tottenham Court Road, London W1P 0LP.

Designed by Celia Floyd
Originated by Dot Gradations Ltd
Printed and bound in Hong Kong/China

04 03 02
10 9 8 7 6 5 4 3 2

ISBN 0 431 01442 6

British Library Cataloguing in Publication Data

Tesar, Jenny
  The planets. – (Space observer) (Take-off!)
  1. Planets – Juvenile literature
  I. Title
  523.4

Acknowledgements

The publishers would like to thank the following for permission to reproduce photographs:
Pages 4-5: ©Blackbirch Press, Inc.; pages 6, 18, 22-23: ©NASA/Science Source/Photo Researchers, Inc.; page 7: A.S.P./Science Source/Photo Researchers, Inc.; pages 8-9, 14: ©Julian Baum/Science Photo Library/Photo Researchers, Inc.; page 10: ©John Foster/Science Source/Photo Researchers, Inc.; page 11: Gazelle Technologies, Inc.; page 12: U.S. Geological Survey/Science Photo Library/Photo Researchers, Inc.; pages 13, 16, 19: ©NASA; page 15: A. Gragera, Latin Stock/Science Photo Library/Photo Researchers, Inc.; page 17: ©NASA/Peter Arnold, Inc.; pages 20, 21: ©W. Kaufmann/JPL/SS/Photo Researchers, Inc.

Cover photograph: Science Photo Library

The Publishers would like to thank Sue Graves for her advice and expertise in the preparation of this book.

Every effort has been made to contact copyright holders of any material reproduced in this book. Any omissions will be rectified in subsequent printings if notice is given to the Publisher.

For more information about Heinemann Library books, or to order, please telephone +44(0)1865 888066, or send a fax to +44(0)1865 314091. You can visit our website at www.heinemann.co.uk

Any words appearing in bold, **like this**, are explained in the Glossary.

Contents

The Solar System 4
Mercury 6
Venus 8
Earth 10
Mars 12
Jupiter 14
Saturn 16
Uranus 18
Neptune 20
Pluto 22
Glossary 24
Index 24

The Solar System

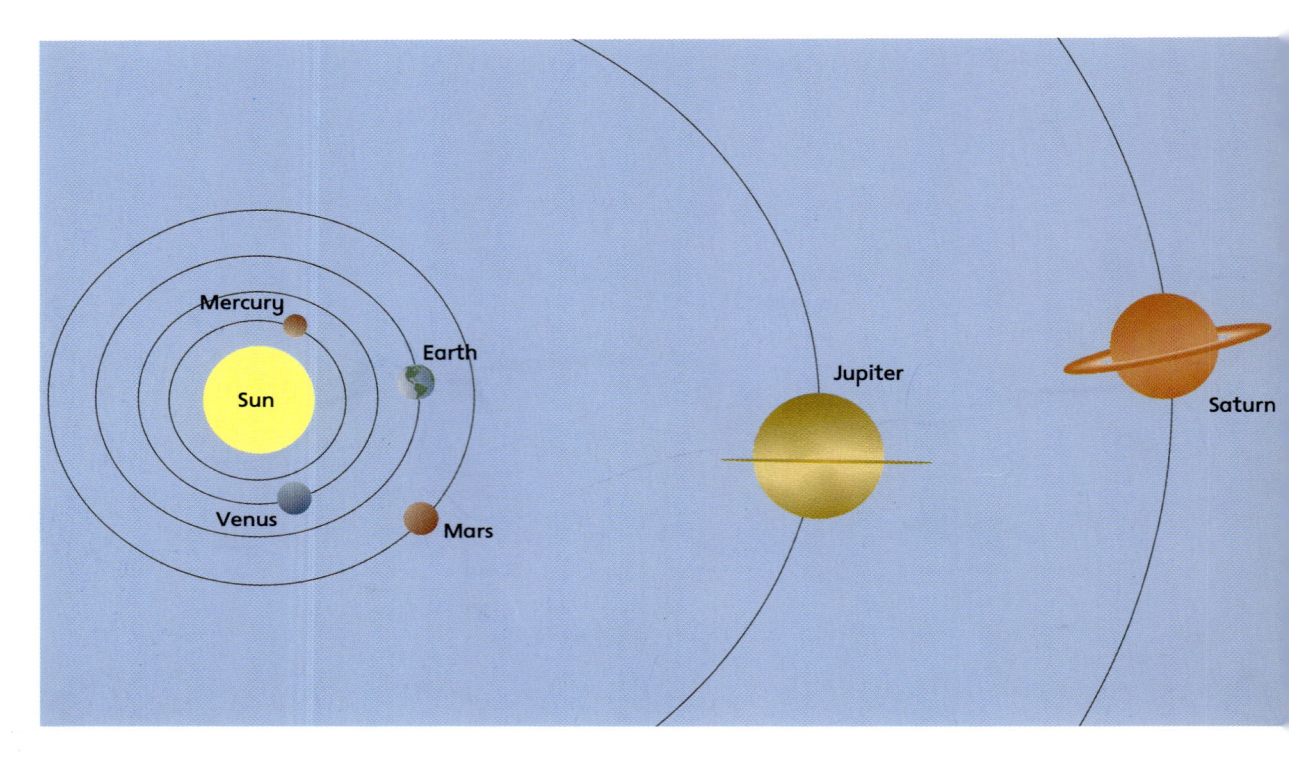

Our Solar System has a Sun and nine planets, including Earth.

Our Earth is part of the Solar System. Solar means sun. The Sun is the centre of our Solar System. The Sun is a huge star.

Scientists think that our Solar System first formed about 4.5 billion years ago!

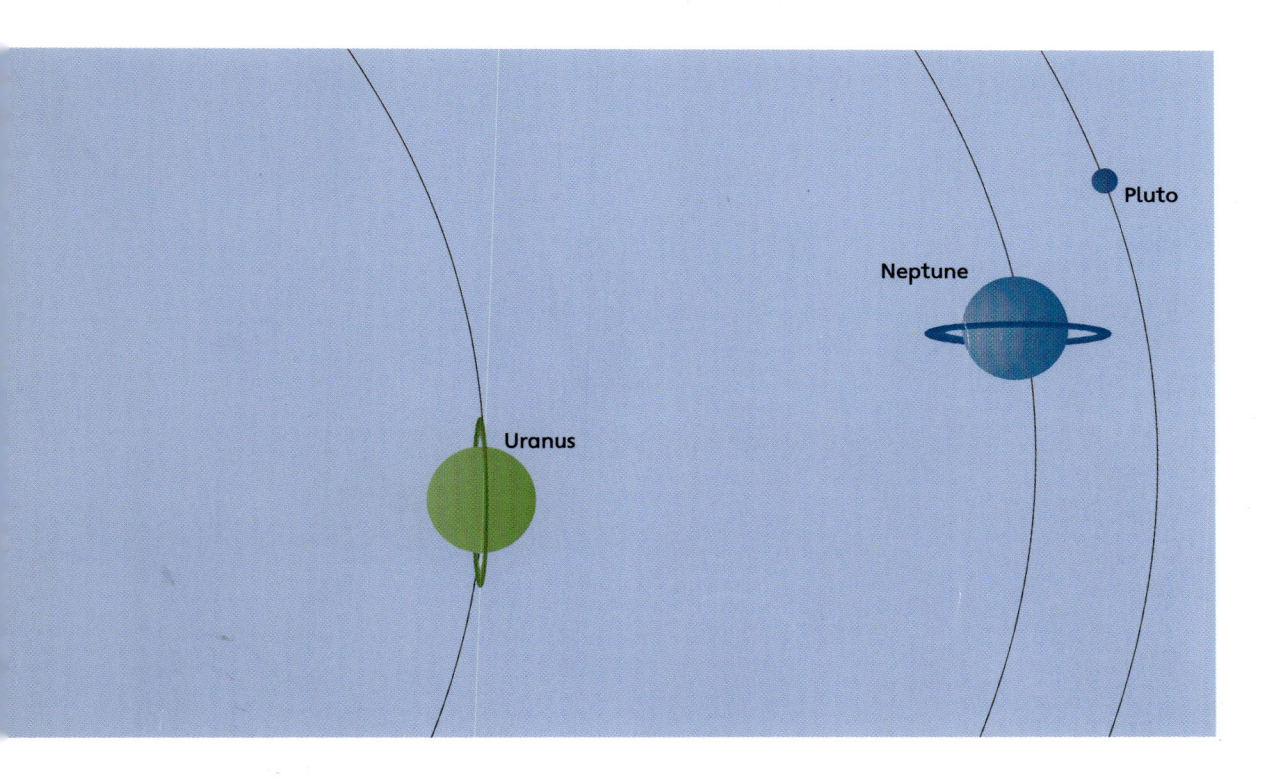

There are nine **planets** in our solar system, including Earth. These planets are ball-shaped. They move around the Sun in paths called **orbits**. Scientists send **probes** to some of the planets to learn about the Solar System.

Mercury

Mercury is:
- 57 million km from the Sun
- the eighth largest planet.

Mercury is the closest **planet** to the Sun. Because Mercury is the closest planet to the Sun, the side that faces the Sun gets very, very hot. It gets so hot that lead could melt there.

Mercury is the closest planet to the Sun.

Mercury's **surface** has craters on it just like our Moon.

crater

Space **probes** were sent into space to find out more about the planets. *Mariner 10* was a probe that visited Mercury. It took pictures that show Mercury looks a lot like our Moon.

Venus

Venus is:
- 107 million km from the Sun
- the sixth largest planet.

Venus is the second **planet** from the Sun. It is the closest planet to Earth. It has no **moons**.

Venus and Earth are about the same size. Thick **acid** clouds always cover Venus. People, animals and plants from Earth couldn't live in this **atmosphere**.

More than 20 **probes** have visited Venus.

An artist's picture of one of the 20 probes that have visited Venus.

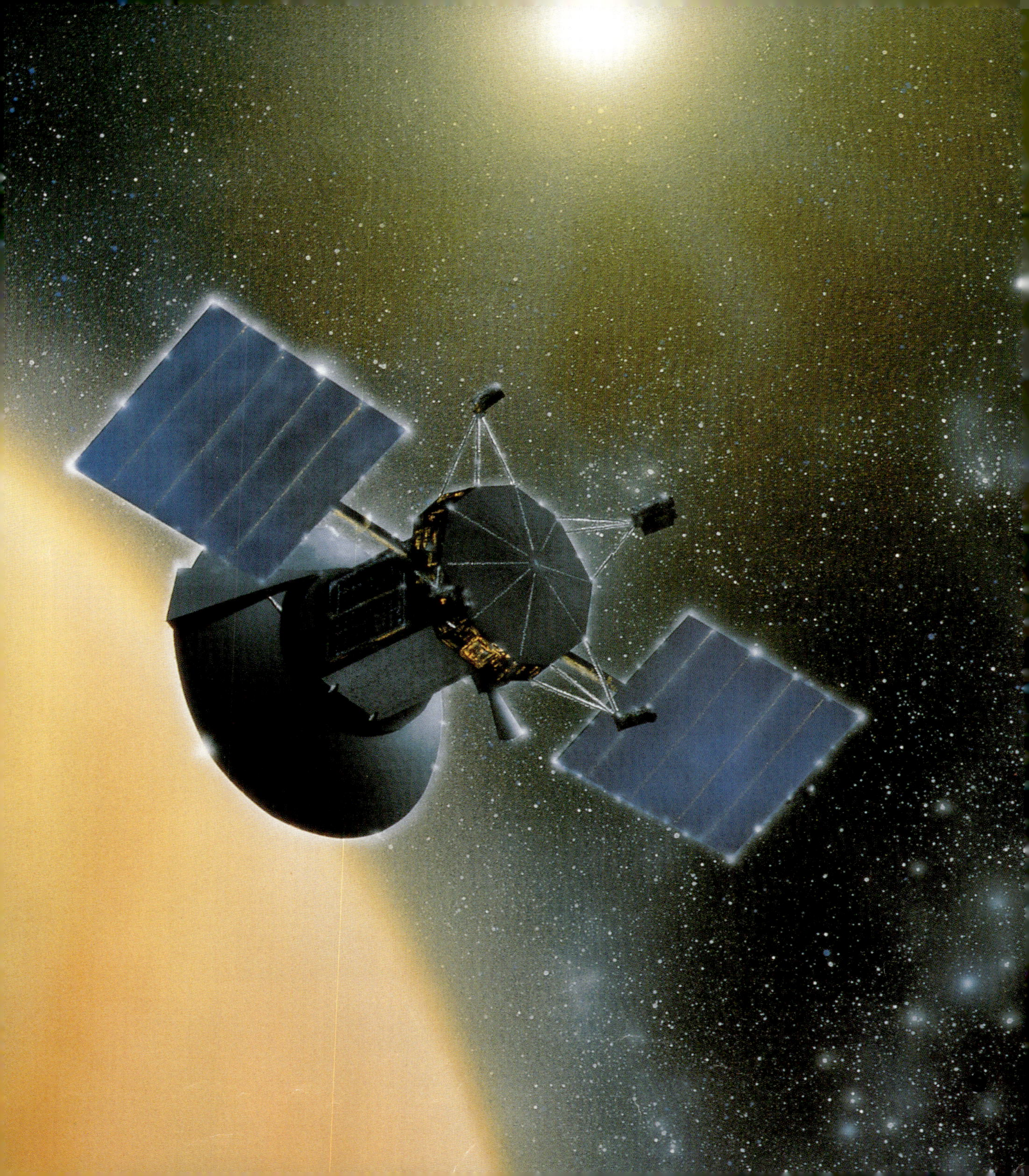

Earth

Earth is:
- 148 million km from the Sun
- the fifth largest planet.

Earth is the third **planet** away from the Sun. It has one **moon** that travels around it. At the same time, the Earth moves around the Sun.

Earth

Moon

The moon is always **orbiting** Earth.

Water covers most of the Earth's surface.

Earth is the only planet that has water on its **surface**. Earth is the only planet where we know there is life.

Water covers nearly three-quarters of the Earth's surface.

Mars

Mars is:
- 227 million km from the Sun
- the seventh largest planet.

Mars is the fourth **planet** from the Sun. It has two **moons**. It is about half the size of Earth.

Mars looks red because the **surface** is covered with red dust.

Mars has large craters shaped like bowls.

Millions of years ago, there was water on Mars. Now it is a dry planet. It is also a very cold one. Many scientists think that there was once life on Mars. In 1997, two **probes** looked at Mars for signs of life.

Jupiter

Jupiter is:
- 774 million km from the Sun
- the largest planet.

Jupiter is the fifth **planet** from the Sun. It has more than 16 **moons**. You could fit all the other planets inside Jupiter and still have extra room!

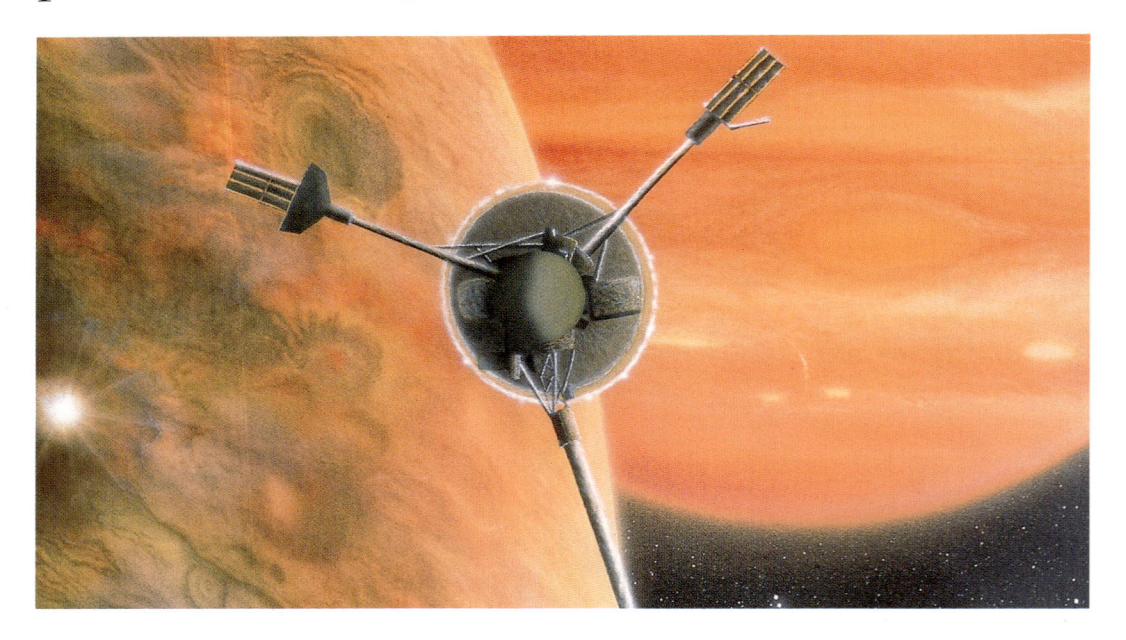

An artist's picture of a probe passing a moon on its way to Jupiter.

red spot

An artist's picture shows Jupiter's rings and some of its moons.

Jupiter is not solid like Earth. It is a huge ball of **gases**. It also has a big red spot on it. Scientists think the spot is a huge storm.

Six **probes** have already visited Jupiter. They discovered thin rings that circle the planet. Scientists think the rings are made of rocks.

15

Saturn

Saturn is:
- 1417 million km from the Sun
- the second largest planet.

Saturn is the sixth **planet** from the Sun. Like Jupiter, it is a giant ball of **gases**.

Saturn is famous for the beautiful rings which circle it. The rings are flat and large.

Saturn's rings are made of billions of pieces of ice and dust.

A picture showing Saturn and some of its many moons.

Saturn has more **moons** than any other planet. In fact it has more than 20 moons! Scientists have sent three **probes** to Saturn to try to find out more about the planet.

17

Uranus

Uranus is:
- 2.7 billion km from the Sun
- the third largest planet.

Uranus is the seventh **planet** from the Sun. Like Jupiter and Saturn, it is also a ball of **gases**. Uranus has more than 15 moons. It also has rings around it, like the other gas planets.

Uranus is a gas planet with dark rings.

An artist's picture shows *Voyager 2* visiting Uranus.

To find out more about Uranus, scientists sent a **probe** called *Voyager 2*. It arrived there in 1986, after visiting Jupiter and Saturn. *Voyager 2* has been the only probe to visit Uranus.

Neptune

Neptune is:
- 4.5 billion km from the Sun
- the fourth largest planet.

Neptune is usually the eighth **planet** from the Sun. But because of its **orbit**, sometimes Pluto is closer to the Sun than Neptune.

Neptune's rings are too thin to show in this photo.

Icy Triton is the largest of Neptune's moons.

Neptune is a **gas** planet. Neptune has more than eight **moons**. The biggest is Triton. Almost half of Triton is covered in ice. It is the coldest place in the Solar System. It even has ice volcanoes!

In 1989, *Voyager 2* became the first **probe** to visit Neptune.

Pluto

Pluto is:
- 5.7 billion km from the Sun
- the smallest planet.

Pluto travels in an unusual **orbit** around the Sun. Usually, Pluto is the farthest **planet** from the Sun. But sometimes, its path crosses Neptune's path. Then Pluto is closer to the Sun – and Neptune is the farthest planet.

> Pluto is not made up of **gases**. It is a frozen ball of rock and ice. Pluto is cold because very little of the Sun's heat reaches it.

Pluto has a **moon** called Charon that circles it.

Glossary

acid a strong substance that can burn your skin
atmosphere layer of gases around a planet
gases substances that spread to fill a space
moon a ball-shaped object that circles a planet
orbit path around the Sun or around another object in space
planet one of nine huge, ball-shaped objects that circle the Sun
probes vehicles without people that are sent to space so that scientists can learn more
surface outside layer of something

Index

Earth   4, 8, 10–11
Jupiter   14–15, 16, 18
Mariner 10 (probe)   7
Mars   12–13
Mercury   6–7
Neptune   20–21, 22
planets, gas   15, 16, 18, 21
Pluto   20, 22
probes   5, 7, 8, 13, 15, 17, 19, 21
Saturn   16–17, 18
Solar System   4, 5
Sun   4
Triton (Neptune's moon)   21
Uranus   18–19
Venus   8
Voyager 2 (probe)   19, 21